microscopic investigations

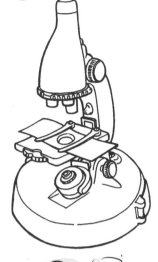

Insects & Spiders

Teaching Guide
Grades 3-6

by Jennifer Boudart

TABLE of CONTENTS

Microscopic Investigations teaching guides are designed to tap into children's natural curiosity about the world they live in. Students informally practice the scientific method every day, as they formulate questions, then design ways to find and communicate answers. *Microscopic Investigations* provides activities that hone scientific inquiry and encourage use of scientific tools. Students use a microscope and associated equipment to explore familiar topics at a new level of detail. Activities focus on minimal preparation and ease of viewing.

Microscopic Investigations: Insects and Spiders offers an up-close look at the tiny animals children encounter every day. Students can study living organisms and prepared specimens to learn more about these small creatures, which represent the most abundant life forms on the planet. In doing so, they are able to practice proper care and handling of animals and work with the tools used to examine them. Units focus on life science concepts highlighted by the National Science Education *Standards*, including characteristics of organisms, life cycles, patterns in ecosystems, adaptation, and animal behavior.

Teaching Guide Features

This *Microscopic Investigations* teaching guide features the following sections, which, progress as magnification increases in each integrated unit.

Teaching Notes include background information and vocabulary terms. They also suggest ways to prepare and present units, assess student learning, and guide students' further exploration.

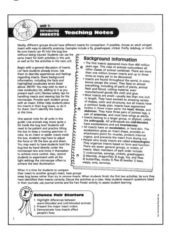

First Look activities direct students to observe general characteristics of specimens, record and interpret what they see, compare their specimens to others, and apply what they have learned to answer related questions in a journal.

Focus On activities explore a specific aspect of the unit topic. Students examine one aspect of a specimen's form or function and analyze its importance.

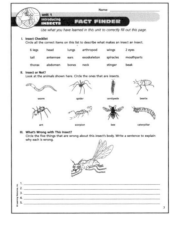

Fact Finder activities challenge students to demonstrate what they have learned by correctly answering questions, labeling structures, and completing statements. These activities may serve as an assessment tool for each unit.

Fact Files throughout the book provide students with a quick-reference study aid. The **Answer Key** on page 32 presents answers to Fact Finder activities.

My Journal is a reproducible page for students to record their research, data, and observations from each activity. Assemble these pages to create an *Investigating Insects & Spiders* journal. Use student journals to assess learning.

INTRODUCTION

microscopic **investigations**

Using a Microscope

The *Microscopic Investigations* series is intended for use with Learning Resources' Quantum® AlphaScope™ Microscope, the Quantum® Big Screen Microscope, or a similar microscope.

The AlphaScope is a medium-power microscope, with magnification levels of 10x, 30x, and 50x. The Big Screen Microscope adjusts to magnifications of 10x, 20x, and 40x. When using an alternate microscope, choose one with similar levels of magnification. In this magnification range, students can observe general characteristics with more distinct features. Students are able to interpret more readily what they're viewing at these levels.

The AlphaScope accommodates prepared slides. It is also equipped with a clear plastic viewing box that holds whole specimens (referred to as the "bug box" in this guide). Viewing live specimens in the bug box is recommended for most activities in this guide.

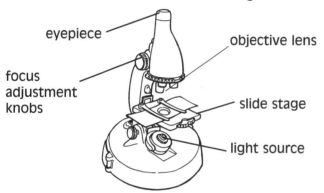

eyepiece

objective lens

focus adjustment knobs

slide stage

light source

With microscopes that do not accommodate a bug box, prepare mounted slide specimens instead. In some cases, you may need to dissect the specimen and mount parts of its anatomy. You may also have to modify activities dealing with animal movement.

Students should be familiar with using the bug box and prepared slides. They should also be able to identify and select the low, medium, and high magnification settings on the microscope. Allow students time to practice using the basic features of a microscope.

Collecting Insects & Spiders

Access to insects and spiders varies with location and time of year. The activities in this guide have been designed with this fact in mind. They are not "species-specific." You may use any species of insect or spider you would like. Have students work in groups to minimize the number of specimens, microscopes, and other equipment required.

Decide if you would like to collect your own insects and spiders. Will you involve students in the process? When in search of your own specimens, bring along an insect net, containers (with lids), and tweezers. Also collect plants from the area where you find each specimen. If you plan to keep insects and spiders for more than one day, you will need to create temporary homes for them. Some activities allow you to use the same insects or spiders for more than one unit.

Tips on collection and handling of insects and spiders are included on the Teaching Notes pages of this book. For additional information about where to find insects and spiders, how to safely collect them, and the care they need, see the list of Further Resources on page 32 of this book.

You may wish to purchase insects and spiders instead of collecting them. Live insects and spiders at all stages of their life cycles are available from several science supply companies.

When you have completed your investigations of insects and spiders, you will have to decide what to do with the specimens. In most cases, you can let them go where you found them. If you have purchased insects or spiders, they may not be native to your area. Letting them go could be harmful or even illegal. In these cases, you can humanely kill the insects by placing them in a refrigerator for several hours.

Ideally, different groups should have different insects for comparison. If possible, choose an adult winged insect with easy-to-identify anatomy. Examples include a fly, grasshopper, cricket, firefly, ladybug, or moth. Be sure insects can fit into the bug box without being injured. Students can use the same insect for both activities in this unit, as well as for the activities in the next unit.

Begin with a general discussion of insects. List facts students already know. Ask them to describe experiences and feelings regarding insects. Share background information, including the facts and highlighted vocabulary terms listed here. (NOTE: You may wish to start a class vocabulary list, adding to it as you present each unit.) Review safety tips for handling insects and viewing tips for the microscope. Provide each student group with an insect. Either help students place the insects in their bug boxes, or do it for them. Don't identify the insects at this time.

One special note for all units in this guide: Live animals may move quite a bit inside the bug box! Students will need to be patient and practice tilting the box to keep a moving specimen in view. As an insect or spider crawls inside the box, students may have to adjust the focus or tilt the box up and down. You may want to have students hold the bug box by hand directly under the microscope lens and move it themselves to achieve more control. Also, remind students to experiment with all the light settings the microscope offers to achieve the best illumination.

Background Information

- The first insects appeared more than 400 million years ago. This class of animals outnumbers all other classes of animal combined. There are more than one million known insects and up to three times as many yet to be discovered.
- Insects are found throughout the world, in every biome except the ocean. They feed on almost everything, including all parts of plants, animal flesh and blood, rotting material, even manufactured goods like cloth and glue.
- Most insects are small—usually less than one inch in length. They have evolved an amazing variety of shapes, color and structures, but all insects have a common body plan. Insects' bodies have three major divisions: the **head**, **thorax**, and **abdomen**. They have three pairs of jointed legs, a pair of **antennae**, and most have wings as adults.
- Insects belong to a larger group, or phylum, called the **arthropods**. All arthropods are **cold-blooded**, have exoskeletons, and are **invertebrates**.
- All insects have an **exoskeleton**, or hard skin. The exoskeleton gives an insect shape, provides an attachment point for muscles, protects internal organs, and prevents the insect from drying out.
- People who study insects are called **entomologists**. They organize insects based on form and function. There are seven general groups, or orders, of insects. Main members of each order include:
  1) cockroaches, earwigs, crickets, grasshoppers
  2) mantids, dragonflies 3) bugs, lice, and fleas
  4) butterflies, moths 5) flies 6) beetles 7) bees, wasps, ants, termites.

When it is time for students to compare their insect to another group's insect, have groups swap bug boxes rather than try to remove insects. When students finish the first two activities, be sure they have identified their insects correctly. Discuss the activities as a class. Help students research questions listed in their journals; use journal entries and the Fact Finder activity to assess student learning.

Science Fair Starters

1. Highlight differences between warm-blooded and cold-blooded animals.
2. Present the major insect orders.
3. Demonstrate how insects affect people's lives.

How do insects differ from other animals?

FACT FILE

1. More than one million insects are known by scientists. Many more have yet to be discovered.
2. Insects are part of a group of animals called **arthropods** *(ARE-throw-podz)*. Animals in this group are cold-blooded: they don't control their own body temperature. They have a hard outer skin called an **exoskeleton** *(EX-oh-SKELL-uh-tin)*. They are **invertebrates** *(in-VERT-uh-brets)*, which means they don't have backbones.
3. All insects' bodies are divided into three main parts: the **head, thorax**, and **abdomen**. All insects have six legs and two feelers, or **antennae** *(an-TEN-uh)*. Most adult insects have wings. Insects also have **compound** eyes with thousands of lenses (humans have only one lens per eye). The lenses help the insect see in all directions and pick up tiny movements.

With your teacher's help, place an insect in your bug box. Place the bug box under your microscope. Set the magnification of your microscope to 10x (or its lowest setting). Locate the insect through your microscope and adjust the focus.

What is the first thing you notice about how your insect looks?

_____

_____

What is the first thing you notice about how your insect acts?

_____

_____

Draw a picture of your insect. Include colors. Label any body parts you know.

For the Record

Answer these questions in your journal. Do your own research, if needed.
- Compare an insect to another kind of animal. How are they different and similar?
- What do you think entomologists try to learn as they study insects?
- What else would you like to learn about insects?

unit 1
Introducing INSECTS

FOCUS ON

Insect Anatomy

How do scientists identify and organize insects?

FACT FILE

1. In general, adult insects have the following body parts, or **anatomy** *(uh-NAT-uh-mee)*:

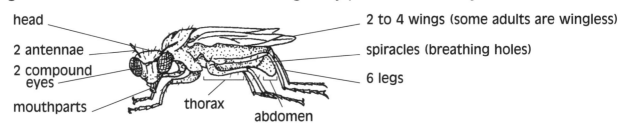

head

2 antennae

2 compound eyes

mouthparts

thorax

abdomen

2 to 4 wings (some adults are wingless)

spiracles (breathing holes)

6 legs

2. Scientists divide insects into seven basic groups. Here are the main members of each:

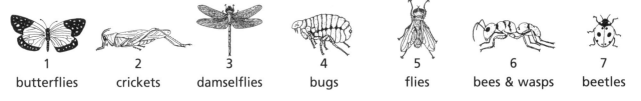

1	2	3	4	5	6	7
butterflies	crickets	damselflies	bugs	flies	bees & wasps	beetles

With your teacher's help, place an insect in your bug box. Place the bug box under your microscope. Set the magnification of your microscope to 30x (or its medium setting). Locate your insect through your microscope, and adjust the focus.

Use the Fact File to identify your insect's body parts. Do any seem to be missing or different from the picture in the Fact File? _____

What is the name of your insect? _____

Which group of insects do you think your insect belongs to and why? _____
_____

Set the magnification to 50x (or its highest setting).
Draw one of your insect's most interesting body parts.
List three words that describe it.

_____ _____ _____

For the Record

Answer these questions in your journal. Do your own research, if needed.
• What else would you like to learn about insect anatomy?
• What do you already know about the insect or insects you studied in this unit?
• What do you think your insect has in common with other insects in its group?

6

unit 1
Introducing INSECTS

FACT FINDER

Use what you have learned in this unit to correctly fill out this page.

I. Insect Checklist
Circle all the correct items on this list to describe what makes an insect an insect.

6 legs	head	lungs	arthropod	wings	2 eyes
tail	antennae	ears	exoskeleton	spiracles	mouthparts
thorax	abdomen	bones	neck	stinger	beak

II. Insect or Not?
Look at the animals shown here. Circle the ones that are insects.

worm

spider

centipede

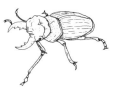

beetle

ant

scorpion

bee

caterpillar

III. What's Wrong With This Insect?
Circle the five things that are wrong about this insect's body. Write a sentence to explain why each is wrong.

1. _____
2. _____
3. _____
4. _____
5. _____

You can use insects collected for Unit 1 for these activities. If possible, give student groups a different insect from those they viewed in Unit 1. You will also need to mount insect wings on slides for students to view. Each group will need two slides featuring two different wings. If you haven't collected dead insects to use, you can refrigerate insects to kill them. Use a tweezers and a scissors if needed to separate each wing and place it on a slide with a cover slip.

Begin the unit by listing what students have learned about insect anatomy. Discuss how body parts vary among insects. Share background information, including the facts and highlighted vocabulary terms listed here. Help students place an insect in their bug boxes, or do it for them. Tell students the name of the insect they will be observing. Remind them to adjust the focus and lighting to achieve the best view, and to hold bug boxes by hand if necessary.

For the Focus On activity, remind students to handle slides carefully, to avoid damaging insect wings. When students have completed the first two activities, discuss them as a class. Help students research questions listed in their journals; use journal entries and the Fact Finder activity to assess student learning.

Background Information

- Insect bodies are divided into the **head, thorax**, and **abdomen**. Eyes, antennae, and mouthparts are found on the head. Wings and legs attach to the thorax. The abdomen contains reproductive organs, breathing organs (**spiracles**), and most of the digestive system.
- *Wings:* Most insects have 2-4 wings as adults. Wings are made of papery **membranes** and are fortified by tubular **veins** which run through them. The membrane may be covered with tiny hairs or **scales**. Some insects have a pair of **elytra**: modified wings that act as protective casings, which cover flight wings when the insect is at rest.
- *Legs:* Insects have six jointed legs, which are modified for climbing, swimming, hopping, crawling, or running. Insect feet are equipped with hooks and hairs; some even have oily pads that work like suction cups. Sensory organs on the feet allow insects to "taste" surfaces they touch.
- *Mouth:* An insect may have a straw-like mouth (called a **proboscis**) to sip liquid nectar; a needle-like, tube-shaped mouth to suck blood or plant juices; a sponge-like mouth to soak up food; or a saw-like mouth with strong jaws to chew, pierce, and cut food. Mouthparts may also be used for grooming and for communication.
- *Eyes:* Insects usually have two eyes, but some may have more, and some may have none. Most insect eyes are **compound**—made up of thousands of lenses that allow them to see in almost all directions and detect the slightest movement. Insect vision is not as clear as human vision, but the eyes do detect patterns, shapes, and differences in light and shade.
- *Antennae:* A pair of antennae acts as an insect's **sensory organs**. They not only provide a sense of touch, but also detect differences in temperature and humidity, feel vibrations, and pick up scents.

Science Fair Starters

1. Make a model of an "anatomically correct" insect.
2. Compare insect mouths, antennae, and legs.
3. Make an "Animal Olympians" chart, listing winners in categories such as fastest, smallest, largest, longest jumper, and so on.

Name: _____

unit 2

Insect ANATOMY   FIRST LOOK

Insect Designs

How is an insect's body designed for its way of life?

FACT FILE

1. Most insects have 2-4 wings as adults. Wings come in many shapes and sizes. They may be see-through and clear or have colors and patterns. Insects may flutter wings slowly or flap them up and down with great speed.
2. Insects have six jointed legs, which they use to climb, swim, hop, crawl, or run. Insect feet have different combinations of hooks, hairs, and sticky pads to grasp different surfaces.
3. An insect's mouth matches its diet. An insect that sucks liquid nectar has a straw-like mouth, called a **proboscis** *(pro-BOSS-iss)*. An insect that sucks blood or plant juices has a needle-like, tube-shaped mouth. An insect that soaks up food has a sponge-like mouth. An insect that chews and tears its food has a saw-like mouth with strong jaws.
4. Insects have a pair of antennae that give them a sense of touch as well as smell. Antennae may look like feathers, fans, horns, strings, and other shapes.

With your teacher's help, place an insect in your bug box.
Write the name of your insect here: _____ .

Place the bug box under your microscope. Set the magnification of your microscope to 10x (or its lowest setting). Locate the insect through your microscope and adjust the focus.

Draw one of your insect's legs.	Draw one of your insect's wings.	Draw your insect's mouthparts.

How does your insect use its legs?	How would you describe your insect's flight?	How do you think the insect's mouthparts work?
_____	_____	_____
_____	_____	_____
_____	_____	_____

For the Record

Answer these questions in your journal. Do your own research, if needed.
- Why do insects look and act differently?
- What are some things it would be difficult for your insect to do, based on its body design?
- What else would you like to learn about the way insects behave?

Name: _____

unit 2

Insect ANATOMY   FOCUS ON   Insect Wings

What do an insect's wings look like up close?

FACT FILE

1. Most adult insects have 2-4 wings, although some don't have any, such as ants.
2. Some insects have one pair of flight wings covered by hard wing cases called **elytra** *(ee-LIE-truh)*.
3. Insect wings are made of paper-thin tissues. They are criss-crossed by **veins**. Blood pumps through these veins, and makes wings stiff and strong.
4. Insect wings may be covered with tiny hairs or **scales**.
5. Color on wings may be created by chemicals the insect makes or by the way light reflects off the wing surface.

With your teacher's help, place two different insect wings on separate prepared slides.

Slide 1: wing from (insect name) _____ flight wing or wing case (circle one)

Slide 2: wing from (insect name) _____ flight wing or wing case (circle one)

Place Slide 1 in your microscope. Set the magnification of your microscope to 30x (or its medium setting). Locate the wing through your microscope, and adjust the focus.

Draw what you see. Include colors and/or patterns.
Also draw the pattern of veins you see.
Label a vein in your drawing.

View Slide 2. Draw what you see.
Include colors and/or patterns.
Also draw the pattern of veins you see.
Label a vein in your drawing.

Slide 1   Slide 2

Set the magnification to 50x (or the highest setting).
View both slides, and draw what you see.
How are the two wings different and similar?

_____
_____
_____
_____

Slide 1   Slide 2

For the Record

Answer these questions in your journal. Do your own research, if needed.
• How do insects move differently when they fly?
• How does an insect compare to other flying animals?
• What else would you like to learn about insect flight?

10

© Learning Resources, Inc.

unit 2

Insect ANATOMY   FACT FINDER

Use what you have learned in this unit to correctly fill out this page.

I. Write About Wings

Fill in the blanks to complete these wing facts.

Most insects have between _____ wings as adults. Insect wings are made of thin tissues. _____ run across the wings to make them strong and stiff. Some insects have elytra, which act as _____. Insects move their wings _____ to fly.

II. Mouth Match-Up

Draw a line to match each mouth to the food it is designed to eat.

fly

blood

ant

soft foods

mosquito

plant leaves

butterfly

flower nectar

III. True or False

Circle the correct answer for each statement.

1. All insects have wings.	T	F
2. Not all insect wings are used for flying.	T	F
3. Antennae can pick up scents.	T	F
4. A proboscis is a saw-like mouth to chew leaves.	T	F
5. Insect eyes are called complex eyes.	T	F
6. Insect wings may be covered with tiny feathers.	T	F

The activities in this unit focus on juvenile stages of insect life cycles (either larva or nymph, depending on which kinds of insects you collect), but be sure to allow time for students to view the egg and chrysalis stages if you're able to obtain specimens. The Focus On activity requires students to view a caterpillar; you can use a caterpillar for the First Look activity as well. Or, you can use mealworms (darkling beetle larvae) purchased from a pet store or science supply company. Caterpillars are common in the spring and fall. You might also use nymphs of such species as the dragonfly (keep them in water).

Whichever species you use, make photocopies of a picture of the insects at the adult stage to provide for the Focus On activity. If you do your own collecting, you will need to identify the species of insect you have. Use a field guide to do this on your own or as a class.

Background Information

- Like all living organisms, insects are born, mature, reproduce, and die. This journey from birth to death is called the **life cycle**. Insect life cycles may take weeks, months, or even years to complete. Generally, adult insects live just long enough to reproduce; some don't even eat.
- Most insects lay eggs. A few species of insects give birth to live young, which have developed from eggs inside their bodies. Insects usually lay large numbers of eggs near a source of food, then leave them to hatch on their own. Some insects care for young as they develop and for a time after they hatch.
- All insects shed their skin, or **molt**, as they grow. The exoskeleton cannot grow to accommodate changes in size. As an insect molts, its skin splits open, and the insect crawls out.
- Insects change form as they grow, a process known as metamorphosis. There are two kinds of **metamorphosis**: complete and incomplete. Most insects undergo complete metamorphosis; incomplete metamorphosis is considered more primitive.
- Insects that undergo **complete metamorphosis** have worm-like bodies when they hatch. They are called **larva**. The larva grows and molts, but maintains its body shape. Then, the larva forms a **chrysalis** (also called a cocoon). Inside its chrysalis, the larva becomes a **pupa**, changing into adult form. It breaks out of the chrysalis as an adult.
- Insects that undergo **incomplete metamorphosis** look like smaller versions of adults when born, except they lack wings, which develop as they grow and molt. At this stage, they are called **nymphs**.
- A caterpillar represents the larval stage of the butterfly/moth life cycle. Compared to an adult, the caterpillar has chewing mouthparts instead of a proboscis, lacks wings, has simple eyes, and has different coloration and protective structures. It does have six true legs (as well as a number of false legs to aid locomotion), and a head, thorax, and abdomen.

Begin the unit by sharing background information, including the facts and highlighted vocabulary terms listed here. Ask students to compare insect growth to the growth of other animals they are familiar with. Once you have given each group an insect and a photocopy to work with, remind them of tips for handling the bug box, and adjusting focus and lighting. Once students have completed the first two activities, discuss them as a class. Help students research questions listed in their journals. Use journal entries and the Fact Finder activity to assess student learning.

Science Fair Starters

1. Care for an insect as it completes its life cycle, documenting the process with photographs.
2. Compare complete versus incomplete metamorphosis.
3. Make a flipbook to tell the story of an insect's life cycle from birth to death.

unit 3
Insect LIFE CYCLES   FIRST LOOK

Metamorphosis

How do insects change as they grow?

FACT FILE

1. As an insect grows, it sheds its exoskeleton, or **molts**.
2. An insect's body changes form as it hatches from an egg and grows into an adult. This change is called **metamorphosis** *(MET-uh-MORF-uh-siss)*.
3. **Incomplete metamorphosis** involves three stages: egg, **nymph** (a smaller, wingless version of an adult), and adult. The nymph grows and sheds its skin, developing adult features.
4. **Complete metamorphosis** involves four stages: egg, **larva** (a worm-like form), **chrysalis** (cocooned stage, with a **pupa** inside), and adult. The larva grows and molts but doesn't change form until it becomes a pupa.
5. Together, the stages of an insect's life are called its **life cycle**.

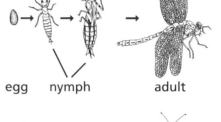

egg   nymph   adult

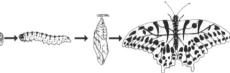

egg   larva   pupa/chrysalis   adult

With your teacher's help, place an insect in your bug box. Write the name of your insect here: _____. Place the bug box under your microscope. Set the magnification of your microscope to 10x (or its lowest setting). Locate the insect through your microscope, and adjust the focus.

Use your Fact File to decide what stage of its life cycle your insect is at: _____

Do you think your insect undergoes incomplete or complete metamorphosis? Explain why.

_____

Draw your insect.
Write three words to describe how it looks.

_____   _____   _____

Compare your insect to the picture your teacher has given you. At what stage of its life cycle is the insect in the picture? _____ How does your insect compare to the insect in the picture? _____

For the Record

Answer these questions in your journal. Do your own research, if needed.
- Which part of an insect's life cycle usually lasts the longest?
- How does a pupa make a chrysalis?
- What else would you like to learn about insect life cycles?

unit 3

Insect LIFE CYCLES   FOCUS ON

Caterpillars

What does the larval stage of a butterfly or moth look like?

FACT FILE

1. Butterflies and moths undergo complete metamorphosis. The common name for a butterfly or moth larva is **caterpillar**.
2. A caterpillar's head has chewing mouthparts and simple eyes.
3. A caterpillar doesn't have wings. It does have six "true" legs attached to its thorax. The rest of its legs are "false legs," or **prolegs**. Prolegs attach to the abdomen. They are chubby and cone-shaped. The tip of each proleg is ringed with hairs surrounding a hook. Prolegs help with crawling and balance.
4. A caterpillar lives to eat! It spends all its time eating and growing. Each time it sheds its skin, it is bigger, but still has the same shape. It will not change form until it encloses itself in a chrysalis. It will become an adult moth or butterfly.

With your teacher's help, place a caterpillar and a leaf or twig in the bug box. Write the name of the caterpillar, if you know it: _____. Place the bug box under your microscope. Set the magnification of your microscope to 30x (or its medium setting). Locate the caterpillar through your microscope, and adjust the focus.

Draw your caterpillar. Include colors.
Label all body parts you can identify.

Identify the caterpillar's true legs and its prolegs.
Draw a single proleg and a single true leg.
How many prolegs does the caterpillar have? _____
Does the caterpillar seem to walk forward all the time? _____

Set the magnification to 50x (or the highest setting).

Identify the caterpillar's head (in front of its true legs).
Draw the caterpillar's head.
Identify its eyes and mouthparts.

For the Record

Answer these questions in your journal. Do your own research, if needed.
- How does the lifestyle of a caterpillar compare to that of an adult butterfly or moth?
- How does a caterpillar survive danger during this stage of its life cycle?
- What else would you like to learn about caterpillars?

Use what you have learned in this unit to correctly fill out this page.

I. Life Cycle Line-Up

For each life cycle, number the pictures from 1 to 4 to place them in the correct order. Also, circle the kind of metamorphosis each picture shows.

complete
metamorphosis
or
incomplete
metamorphosis

_____   _____   _____   _____

complete
metamorphosis
or
incomplete
metamorphosis

_____   _____   _____   _____

II. Label the Caterpillar

Label the following parts of this caterpillar: true leg, proleg, head, thorax, abdomen, mouthparts, eye. Also, label what stage of its life cycle the caterpillar is in.

_____

_____

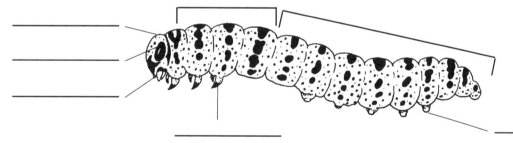

_____   life cycle stage

_____   _____

III. Write About Life Cycles

Fill in the blanks to complete these life cycle facts.

Most insects start life inside _____. As an insect grows, it sheds its skin to _____. It also changes form. This change is called _____. Complete metamorphosis involves _____ stages. Insects that go through complete metamorphosis are called _____ when they hatch. They do not develop adult parts until they become _____. Incomplete metamorphosis involves _____ stages. Insects that go through incomplete metamorphosis are called _____ when they hatch. Nymphs look like adults without _____.

Since every insect is adapted in some way for survival, whichever species you choose should fit this activity. Ideally, the insect's survival mechanisms will be easy to identify and will fall into the general categories listed in the background information. Some insects make excellent examples of survival mechanisms, including bees (stingers, colony living), ladybugs (warning coloration), and katydids (camouflage).

Begin the unit with a discussion about what living organisms need to survive. Ask students to share what they know about how animals get the things they need to survive. Discuss dangers that threaten an insect's survival. Share background information, including the facts and highlighted vocabulary terms listed here.

The Focus On activity challenges students to "activate" a survival mechanism in some way. Help students decide ways in which to do this. They might place plant material for a camouflaged animal to hide in. They might place another insect in the box to make the insect feel threatened. They might place a bit of food in the box.

Background Information

- All living organisms need food, shelter, and water to survive. They must also defend themselves against life-threatening events, such as being killed by a predator or while fighting with others, weather events, and so on.
- Part of an animal's survival success includes its ability to reproduce, raising young that live to reproduce themselves.
- Animals have **adaptations** that increase their survival success. An adaptation is any behavior or physiological feature that helps an animal find food and water, defend itself, shelter itself, and reproduce. Adaptations are the result of evolution, and take many generations to emerge.
- Insects have countless adaptations to aid survival. These adaptations fall into a variety of categories:
  escape: being able to run, fly, or swim away from danger.
  weapons: stingers, bites, chemical sprays, spines, jaws, hard shells, and other physical features that help insects with attack or defense.
  protective coloring: **camouflage**, **mimicry** (having a shape or pattern of colors that mimics another animal or an object, such as a leaf), warning coloration (bright colors that signal defenses such as tasting bad or being poisonous).
  living together: forming groups to share tasks such as finding food, defense, caring for young, and maintaining a shelter.
  hibernation or migration: becoming inactive or traveling to escape harsh weather.
  having large families: laying hundreds or even thousands of eggs.
- Every aspect of an insect's anatomy and behavior can be linked to its survival.

When students have completed the first two activities, discuss results as a class. Help students research questions listed in their journals; use journal entries and the Fact Finder activity to assess student learning.

Science Fair Starters

1. Make a "First Aid for Insect Attacks" display, covering topics such as allergies, bites, and stings.
2. Collect a few insects that use camouflage for protection. Create a display with the specimens, setting them against their natural backgrounds to highlight this survival mechanism.
3. Create a display about the life cycle of the 17-year periodic cicada, one of the insect world's super survivors.

unit 4

Insect SURVIVAL **FIRST LOOK**

How do insects keep themselves alive?

FACT FILE

1. Insects, and all animals, face danger to their lives every day. They must find food to eat and water to drink. They need shelter from the weather. They must protect themselves from other animals that want to eat them or fight with them. They must be able to reproduce.

2. Insects have **adaptations** *(ad-ap-TAY-shuns)* to help protect and feed themselves, and to reproduce. An adaptation is something about the way an insect acts or how its body works which helps it survive. It takes many insect lifetimes for an adaptation to develop.

3. An adaptation may be tied to:
   a. the way an insect acts to attack or defend itself.
   b. how an insect's body functions: its senses, its method of getting around, its coloring, and so on.
   c. the way an insect deals with danger: by fighting or escaping.
   d. the way an insect reproduces, such as laying lots of eggs or protecting them from danger.

With your teacher's help, place an insect in your bug box. Write the name of your insect here: _____. Set the magnification of your microscope to 10x (or its lowest setting). Locate the insect through your microscope, and adjust the focus.

Watch your insect for a few minutes. Describe how you think its behavior might help it survive.

_____

Look at your insect's body design. Describe how you think the insect's body helps it survive.

_____

Do you think your insect would choose to fight or escape if danger were near? Explain why.

_____

Compare your insect to another group's insect. How are their adaptations different and similar?

_____

For the Record

Answer these questions in your journal. Do your own research, if needed.
- Review earlier activities you have done with insects. What examples can you find of how those insects had adaptations for survival?
- How do people feel about insect's survival adaptations?
- What else would you like to learn about insect survival?

unit 4

Name: _____

I n s e c t
SURVIVAL   **FOCUS ON**

Insect Attack
and Defense

What are some common forms of insect defense and attack?

FACT FILE

1. Insects have countless adaptations, but they do fit into some general groups:
   a. *escape*: being able to run, fly, or swim away from danger.
   b. *weapons*: stingers, bites, chemical sprays, spines, jaws, hard shells, and other anatomy or behavior that helps insects with attack or defense.
   c. *protective coloring*: **camouflage** *(KAM-oh-flahj)* helps an animal blend in with its surroundings; **mimicry** *(MIM-ik-ree)* means having a shape or pattern of colors that copies another animal or an object, like a leaf; **warning colors** (bright colors that warn predators that an insect tastes bad, is poisonous, or has another weapon.
   d. *living together*: forming groups to share tasks such as finding food, defense, caring for young, and maintaining a shelter.
   e. *hibernation or migration*: becoming inactive or traveling to escape harsh weather.
   f. *having large families:* laying hundreds or even thousands of eggs.

Use the same insect from the First Look activity. Place the bug box under your microscope. Set the magnification of your microscope to 30x (or its medium setting). Locate the insect through your microscope, and adjust the focus.

Look carefully at your insect. Use the Fact File list to make guesses about which kinds of survival adaptations your insect might use. List them here:

_____

_____

Draw and describe one of your insect's survival adaptations.

_____

With your teacher's help, think of a way you might get your insect to attack or defend itself. Describe your plan here:

_____

_____

Change the magnification of your microscope to 10x (or its lowest setting). Try out your idea with your insect. Write about what happens. _____

For the Record

Answer these questions in your journal. Do your own research, if needed.
- What did this activity teach you about insect attacks or defense?
- If you could have tried any trick to get your insect to show off its adaptations for survival, what would it have been?
- What else would you like to learn about insect attack and defense?

Insects
SURVIVAL   FACT FINDER

Use what you have learned in this unit to correctly fill out this page.

Name: _____

I. Insect Survival Circle-It

Circle the correct answers for the following statements.

1. Nature's way of helping insects survive is called:

    a. animation   b. adaptation   c. life cycle   d. none of these

2. Examples of survival tricks insects use include:

    a. hibernation   b. chemical sprays   c. mimicry   d. all of these

3. Camouflage is a survival trick that helps an animal:

    a. blend in   b. look like something else
    c. warn others to stay away   d. all of these

4. Laying eggs that hatch into young is called:

    a. migration   b. defense   c. reproduction   d. life cycle

II. Survival Tactic Match-Up

Draw a line to match each picture to the survival adaptation that describes it.

1.    reproduction

2.    camouflage

3.    escape

4.    body weapon

III. Survival Portrait

Draw a picture of an imaginary insect that defends itself in the following ways: uses a body part designed as a weapon, has warning coloring, and can see very well. Also, label each defense.

You can purchase aquatic insects for this activity, or collect them yourself. Any spot with standing water will provide a variety of insects to study. If you're lucky, you will be able to net individual specimens. Look for larger insects skimming on the surface, diving, or clinging to rocks. You can also scoop up a mixture of water, plants and material such as rocks, sand and muck. Allow these materials to settle, and you will be able to see which insects are present in your water sample. Collect extra water to fill a holding tank for your insects as you conduct this unit. You will likely not know which kinds of insects you have without using a field guide. Keep one handy for students to use in identifying insects during their activities.

Begin this unit with a discussion of habitats: what they are, examples of different habitat types, and what makes good habitat for an animal to live in. Discuss aquatic habitats, such as wetlands, and ask students to name any insects they know that live in or around water. Share background information, including the facts and highlighted vocabulary terms listed here. Have students cover any airholes in the bug box with tape, to prevent leaking. Then, fill each group's box with a bit of water from the holding tank. The water should contain several animals; plant material is fine, too. Remind students of tips for handling the bug box and adjusting focus and lighting.

Background Information

- All insects have a need for water. They require water to drink. They may lay their eggs in water. They may live underwater before becoming adults. They may even spend their entire life cycles in this environment.
- Insects that live in water **habitats** are called **aquatic** insects.
- Insects make use of all water "zones": skimming and clinging to the water's surface, swimming and diving through the depths, or crawling along the water's bottom.
- Aquatic insects must take in oxygen, just like their terrestrial counterparts. Some insects take in air at the water's surface through their spiracles or a tube at the tip of the abdomen, and return when they need more. Others carry a bubble of air at the tip of the abdomen or tucked under a wing, like a SCUBA tank. Yet others have **gills** to remove oxygen from the water.
- Aquatic insects are dull-colored, to blend with their surroundings. Some aquatic insects are **carnivores**, some are **herbivores**, and some are **scavengers**.

As students complete the First Look activity, help them to decide which animals they see are insects and which are not. For the Focus On activity, help students to isolate a single insect for study. Encourage them to use a field guide to identify their species of insect, as well as whether it is a larva, nymph, or adult. When students have completed the first two activities, discuss results as a class. Help students research questions listed in their journals; use journal entries and the Fact Finder activity to assess student learning.

Science Fair Starters

1. Make a display about aquatic insect life at different levels within the water column. Use one sheet of poster board for each level: surface, middle, bottom. Then, tape the pieces together to make a circular column.
2. Set up an aquarium, along with a key to the aquatic insects that live in it.
3. Make an exhibit about the life of a dragonfly, in and out of water.

How do insects live underwater?

FACT FILE

1. All insects use water in some way, even if only to drink.
2. Many insects lay their eggs in water. The young that hatch from these eggs may spend part or all of their life cycles underwater. Some insects leave water to become adults, while others choose to spend most of their time in the water.
3. Insects that live in water are called **aquatic** *(uh-KWAH-tik)* insects.
4. Insects make use of all water "zones." Some skate along the water's surface or hang just beneath it. Others swim and dive through the water. Still others crawl along the water's bottom.
5. Most aquatic insects hunt other animals. A few eat plants, though, and some are scavengers.

With your teacher's help, fill a bug box with a water sample and seal it. Place the bug box under your microscope. Set the magnification of your microscope to 10x (or its lowest setting). Locate the spider through your microscope, and adjust the focus.

What is the first thing you notice about the water in your bug box? _____

_____

Do you think all the creatures in the water are insects? What other kinds of animals might you be seeing? _____

_____

How many creatures can you count in your water sample? _____

Describe the movements of the animals in your water sample. _____

_____

Compare your water sample to another group's water sample. How are they different and similar? _____

_____

_____

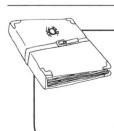

For the Record

Answer these questions in your journal. Do your own research, if needed.
- What surprised you the most about your water sample?
- What role do you think aquatic insects play in a water habitat?
- What else would you like to learn about water habitats?

Name: _____

unit 5

W a t e r
INSECTS

FOCUS ON

Aquatic
Adaptations

How is an aquatic insect's body designed for its way of life?

FACT FILE

1. Life in water is different than life on land. Underwater, it's harder to get oxygen. It's harder to see. On the other hand, it can be easier to move around. Vibrations also travel easier through water.
2. Aquatic insects must take in oxygen. Some insects take in air at the water's surface through their spiracles or a tube at the tip of the abdomen. They must return to the surface for more air when they run out. Other insects carry a bubble of air at the tip of the abdomen or tucked under a wing, like a SCUBA tank. They, too, make trips to the surface for air refills. Some insects have gills, which remove oxygen from the water.
3. Aquatic insects are dull-colored, to blend in with their surroundings.
4. Insects that move along the water's surface are lightweight. They have long legs tipped with hairs and oil to avoid sinking through the water's surface.
5. Insects that swim often have long, strong legs to push through the water. Some insects shoot out a burst of air from the abdomen. This pushes them through the water at great speed.

With your teacher's help, choose one water insect to place in your bug box. Write the name of the insect here, if you know it: _____. Place the bug box under your microscope. Set the magnification of your microscope to 30x (or its medium setting). Locate the aquatic insect through your microscope, and adjust the focus.

Draw the insect. Include colors.
Label all body parts you know.

Describe how your insect moves and if it stays at the surface, in the middle, or at the bottom of the water. _____

How does your insect's body seem to be designed for a life in water? _____

_____

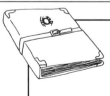

For the Record

Answer these questions in your journal. Do your own research, if needed.
• Why do so many insects lay their eggs in water?
• What do aquatic insects do in winter, especially if water freezes?
• What else would you like to learn about aquatic insect behavior?

unit 5

Water INSECTS FACT FINDER

Use what you have learned in this unit to correctly fill out this page.

I. True or False
Circle the correct answer for each statement.

1. Insects that live in water are called aquatic insects.   T   F
2. Insects do not live underwater once they become adults.   T   F
3. Insects that live underwater do not take in oxygen.   T   F
4. Water insects can only be found at the water's surface.   T   F
5. Many insects lay their eggs in water.   T   F

II. Aquatic Adaptations
Look at each water insect. Decide if it lives on top of the water, swims through the water, or stays on the bottom. Think about what adaptations have evolved for each insect. Match each insect with the correct description.

1.

A. I am a caddisworm. I live on the bottom of watery areas. My coloring helps me blend in with my surroundings and my hard case protects me from predators.

2.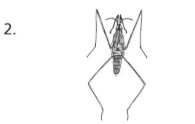

B. I am a diving beetle. I swim through the middle of my watery home, and carry air bubbles with me so that I can breath underwater.

3.

C. I am a water boatman. My long, strong legs help me to swim or paddle in the middle of my watery home.

4.

D. I am a water strider. I have very long legs that spread out the weight of my body and allow me to skim along the surface of the water.

III. My Day Down Under
Use this space to write a short story about what your day might be like if you were an aquatic insect. _____

_____

_____

_____

_____

The spiders you use for this unit can also be used for the First Look activity in the next unit. Spiders are easy to locate year-round; they take up residence indoors and can be found lurking in corners of windowsills, walls, or in the garage. If you collect your own spiders, you may wish to collect web samples for Unit 7 at the same time (see Teaching Notes, page 28). Also collect any egg sacs you find for students to observe after they complete their activities. Though chances are very slim, you should find out if you might encounter any poisonous spiders in your area, such as the brown recluse spider or the black widow spider.

When choosing spiders to collect, try to find large ones, as small ones simply move too fast for students to track with their microscopes. You might also want to collect bits of bark or leaves to place in the bug boxes; spiders will crouch on them, making them easier for students to study. Begin the unit with a general discussion of spiders. Make a list of what students know about spiders. Ask students to describe how they feel about spiders and to share any experiences they may have had with them. Point out that spiders have the important job of keeping insect numbers under control.
Share background information, including the facts and vocabulary listed here. Place spiders in the bug boxes for students, to minimize chances of escape.

Background Information

- Spiders belong to a class of animals called **arachnids**, which also includes scorpions, ticks, and others. There are more than 30,000 species of spiders. Like insects, spiders have been highly successful colonizers and live everywhere except Antarctica.
- Spiders are often mistaken for insects. Like insects, spiders are arthropods. However, spiders do not have wings or antennae. They have eight legs and two main body parts: a combined head and thorax region called the **cephalothorax** *(SEFF-uh-low-THOR-ax)* and an **abdomen**. The two sections are linked by a narrow waist. The cephalothorax is covered with a hardened shield called a **carapace**.
- The spider's head has a pair of jaws, called **chelicerae**. Behind these is the mouth. A pair of sensory organs called the **pedipalps** flanks the mouth. Nearly all spiders have poison glands. Spiders do not chew their food. Instead, they paralyze prey and deliver juices that turn body tissues into liquids that can be sucked up.
- Most spiders have eight eyes, but some have four or six. Spiders have an additional pair of visual structures, called **ocilli**, which detect changes in light. Despite having numerous eyes, spiders have poor vision.
- The spider's legs attach to the cephalothorax. They are jointed, forming three segments, and they are tipped with two claws, which help with grasping.
- The spider's abdomen contains most of the digestive and reproductive organs, as well as silk-making organs.
- A spider's body is covered in hair, spines and bristles collectively called **setae**, which help sense their environment. The sense of touch is a spider's main method of investigating its surroundings.
- Spiders hatch from eggs, and are called **spiderlings**. They molt as they grow.

Once students have completed their activities, discuss results as a class. Help students research questions listed in their journals; use journal entries and the Fact Finder activity to assess student learning.

Science Fair Starters

1. Make an "anatomically correct" spider model.
2. Create a model of spiderlings hatching out of an egg sac.
3. Share myths and misconceptions surrounding spiders.

unit 6

Spider ANATOMY FIRST LOOK

Spider Anatomy

How do spiders differ from other animals?

FACT FILE

1. Spiders are arthropods, like insects. Spiders also belong to a group of animals called **arachnids**, which includes scorpions, ticks, and others. There are more than 30,000 species of spiders.
2. Spiders have two main body parts: the **cephalothorax** *(SEFF-uh-low-THOR-ax)* and **abdomen**. The cephalothorax is covered with a hard shield called a **carapace** *(CARE-uh-pace)*.
3. Spiders have eight legs, each tipped with two or three claws.
4. Spiders are covered with sensitive hairs of different lengths and thicknesses.
5. Spiders hatch from eggs and are called **spiderlings**. They molt as they grow.

carapace

abdomen

cephalothorax

With your teacher's help, place a spider in your bug box. Write the name of the spider here, if you know it: _____. Place the bug box under your microscope. Set the magnification of your microscope to 10x (or its lowest setting). Locate the spider through your microscope, and adjust the focus.

What is the first thing you notice about the spider? _____

_____

Draw the spider. Include colors.
Label all body parts you can identify.
Write three words to describe the spider.

_____ _____ _____

Watch the spider move. Which directions can it go? How do its legs move—one at a time or in pairs? Does the spider seem to use its legs for anything other than walking? _____

_____

Compare your spider to another group's spider. How are they different and similar? _____

_____

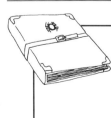

For the Record

Answer these questions in your journal. Do your own research, if needed.
• What surprised you most about your spider's body? Its behavior?
• How does a spider's body compare to an insect's body?
• What else would you like to learn about spider anatomy?

unit 6

S p i d e r ANATOMY **FOCUS ON** **Spider Head**

What does a spider's face look like?

FACT FILE

1. Most spiders have eight eyes, but some have four or six. The size and arrangement of eyes differs from spider to spider. Even with its many eyes, a spider has poor eyesight.
2. A spider has two **ocilli** *(oss-IH-lee)* on top of its head, which sense changes in light.
3. A spider's mouth is small. It is covered by two curved, hairy structures called **chelicerae** *(chel-ISS-uh-ray)*. The chelicerae are tipped with poisonous fangs. They are used in feeding, defense, and sometimes for digging.
4. Spiders are carnivores, but they can't chew food. Instead, they coat prey with digestive juices, which turn it into a liquid the spider sucks up.
5. On either side of mouth are leg-like **pedipalps**, which are used for touching and tasting.

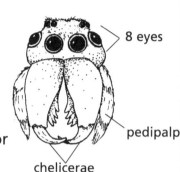

8 eyes

pedipalp

chelicerae

Use the spider from the First Look activity in this unit. Write the name of the spider here, if you know it: _____. Place the bug box under your microscope. Set the magnification of your microscope to 30x (or its medium setting). Locate the spider through your microscope, and adjust the focus.

How many eyes do you see? _____ Are all the eyes the same size? _____

Look at the spider's pedipalps. How does the spider move them? _____

_____

Draw your spider's face.
Label all body parts you know.

Set the magnification to 50x (or the highest setting.) Position the bug box so you can see the spider from below. Try to identify the spider's chelicerae and its mouth. Gently tap on the bug box as you watch the spider. How does it react? _____

_____

For the Record

Answer these questions in your journal. Do your own research, if needed.
- What kind of view do you think a spider sees through its eyes?
- What other animals use poison to kill their prey?
- What else would you like to learn about a spider's vision or feeding habits?

unit 6

Spider ANATOMY — FACT FINDER

Use what you have learned in this unit to correctly fill out this page.

Name: _____

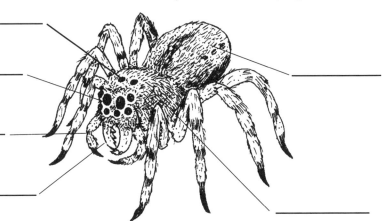

I. Spider Portrait
Label the following body parts on this spider portrait: cephalothorax, abdomen, chelicerae, ocilli, pedipalp, eye.

II. Spider Fact Circle-It
Circle the correct answer for each question.

1. Spiders are invertebrates, meaning they do not have:
   a. backbones   b. teeth   c. horns   d. none of these

2. Spiders depend mainly on their sense of:
   a. smell   b. touch   c. sight   d. hearing

3. The number of spider species in the world is about:
   a. 5,000   b. 100   c. 30,000   d. 100,000

4. Spiders belong to a group of animals called:
   a. arachnids   b. spidera   c. archifroms   d. none of these

III. Insect and Spider Table
Compare how insects and spiders are alike and different.

	Insects	Spiders
Number of legs		
Number of body sections		
Common number of eyes		
Wings? (Yes or No)		
Exoskeleton? (Yes or No)		
Antennae? (Yes or No)		
Molt to grow? (Yes or No)		
Name of young when hatched		
Arthropod? (Yes or No)		

© Learning Resources, Inc.

27

SPIDER BEHAVIOR
Teaching Notes

You can use spiders from the last unit for the First Look activity. You will also need to mount spider web samples on slides for each group to observe. Collect a variety of webs, and try to include any debris they might contain. To collect pieces of web, locate a web, and be sure the spider is not present. Gently sweep a glass slide against the web to tear it. The strands of the web will naturally cling to the glass. Don't place a cover slip on the slide. You will also need to provide student groups with tweezers and bits of light material to sprinkle on their web strands.

Begin by sharing information, including the facts and vocabulary listed here. Ask students how they think spiders know how to spin webs, and share illustrations you may have of how an orb weaver makes its web. Ask students where they have seen webs, and if they have ever watched a spider at work in one. Once again, place spiders in bug boxes for students, to minimize chances of escape; also give student groups the other items mentioned above. When students complete the first two activities, discuss results as a class. Help students answer the questions listed in their journals; use journal entries and the Fact Finder activity to assess student learning.

Background Information

- **Silk** is a special kind of protein made inside a spider's body. All spiders make silk and use it for different purposes, including weaving **webs**, spinning **egg sacs**, immobilizing prey, and locomotion.
- Silk flows from a spider's body through its **spinnerets**. Spinnerets are hollow, finger-like tips at the back of the abdomen. A spider draws silk out from its spinnerets with its legs.
- Silk may be thick, thin, slippery, sticky, or stringy, depending on how it's used. A spider can alter the thickness and stickiness of the silk it's spinning.
- Spiders can hang from a strand of silk, called a **dragline**. They can let out a dragline to drop quickly through the air, then climb back up it again. Young spiders, or spiderlings, may use ballooning to travel: they release a dragline that catches the air and allows them to float to a new home.
- The classic spider web is an **orb web**: a pattern of circles crossed by "spokes" like those on a bicycle wheel. The circles are made of sticky thread to catch insects. Spiders also make **tangle webs** from a random assortment of threads and **sheet webs** from smooth sheets of silk.
- A spider waits for vibrations in the web to alert it to the presence of a trapped insect. It rushes across the web to immobilize the prey. The spider can walk across the web by avoiding sticky strands, and with the help of hooks and oily pads on its feet.
- Spider webs can support a spider and snag insects that weigh hundreds or even thousands of times what the web does. Still, spiders have to repair or even rebuild their webs daily.

Science Fair Starters

1. Create a guide to help others find and identify spider webs.
2. Make a model of an orb web, and outline the steps a spider goes through to build one.
3. Document the process of a spider building its web using photographs.

unit 7
Spider BEHAVIOR FIRST LOOK

How does a spider make silk?

FACT FILE

1. **Silk** is a special kind of protein made inside a spider's body. All spiders make silk.
2. Silk flows from a spider's body through its **spinnerets**. Spinnerets are hollow, finger-like tips at the back of the abdomen. A spider draws silk out from its spinnerets with its legs.
3. Spider silk has different uses. Spiders can hang from a strand of silk called a **dragline**. They can weave silk into webs. They can form silk sacs for their eggs or make silk linings for their nests. Spiders can also wrap up insects they trap in their webs.
4. Spiders make different kinds of silk depending on how they plan to use it. Silk may be thick, thin, sticky, or smooth. All silk is amazingly strong: One silk thread is stronger than a steel thread of the same thickness.

With your teacher's help, place a spider in your bug box. Write the name of the spider, if you know it: _____. Place the bug box under your microscope. Set the magnification of your microscope to 10x (or its lowest setting). Locate the spider through your microscope, and adjust the focus.

Look at the spider's abdomen.
Locate the spinnerets at the tip of the abdomen.
Draw what you see.

Describe any silk you might see around the

spinnerets. _____

With your teacher's help, mount silk threads from a spider's web on a prepared slide. Place the slide on the microscope, and focus to view it. Draw what you see. Write three words to describe the silk threads.

_____ _____ _____

Gently pull at a silk strand with a tweezers. Gently shake a bit of pepper, bits of leaf, or some other small, light material onto the silk threads. What do you notice about the silk?

_____

For the Record

Answer these questions in your journal. Do your own research, if needed.
- How have you seen a spider put its silk to work?
- Do any other animals make silk?
- What else would you like to learn about spider silk?

unit 7

S p i d e r
BEHAVIOR   **FOCUS ON**

Webs

What does a spider web look like up close?

FACT FILE

1. All spiders trap and eat live prey. Not all spiders build webs. Some use speed to grab insects, while others hide in underground tunnels.
2. The most familiar kind of spider web is an **orb web**: a pattern of circles crossed by "spokes" like those on a bicycle wheel. The circles are made of sticky thread to catch insects.
3. Two other common web designs are the **tangle web**, made from a jumble of threads, and the **sheet web**, made from layers of smooth silk.
4. When the web traps an insect, the threads shake. This is the signal for the spider to rush across the web. It grabs the insect with its fangs.
5. A spider can walk across its web by avoiding sticky strands. It also has hooks and oily pads on its feet to keep it from getting stuck.

Use the slide you prepared for the First Look activity. Place the slide under your microscope. Set the magnification of your microscope to 30x (or its medium setting). Locate the silk threads through your microscope, and adjust the focus.

Draw what you see.

Do you see anything else on the slide? What do you think may be mixed in with the silk strands? _____

_____

_____

What kind of web do you think this sample comes from? Why do you think so?

_____

_____

Set the magnification to 50x (or the highest setting.)
Do all the silk strands look the same? If not, explain how they are different.

_____

For the Record

Answer these questions in your journal. Do your own research, if needed.
• Have you ever walked into a spider web? How did it feel?
• Where do you usually see spider webs?
• What else would you like to learn about spider webs?

unit 7
Spider BEHAVIOR   FACT FINDER

Use what you have learned in this unit to correctly fill out this page.

I. Write About Silk
Fill in the blanks to complete these silk facts.

Silk is made by _____ spiders. Silk leaves a spider's body through organs called _____. These organs are located at the tip of the spider's_____. Spiders use silk to make _____ sacs. They also weave silk into _____. Spiders can hang from a strand of silk called a _____.

II. True or False
Circle the correct answer for each statement.

1. The most familiar kind of spider web is an orb web.   T   F
2. Spiders spin one kind of silk, which is sticky.   T   F
3. All spiders weave webs to trap insects.   T   F
4. Spiders can walk across their webs without getting stuck.   T   F
5. Some spiders eat plants instead of insects.   T   F

III. Weave a Web
Read each sentence. Draw the kind of web you think each spider makes.
Label each kind of web you draw.

I don't use a special design when weaving my web, which is also called a cobweb.

My web is a beautiful combination of straight lines and circles. Some of my threads are very sticky.

My web is flat and smooth. I place my threads in many straight lines.

_____ web   _____ web   _____ web

Unit 1: Introducing Insects   Page 7
I. Insect Checklist
6 legs, head, arthropod, wings, 2 eyes, antennae, exoskeleton, spiracles, mouthparts, thorax, abdomen
II. Insect or Not?
beetle, ant, bee, caterpillar
III. What's Wrong with This Insect?
Antennae should be on head. Insect eyes are compound. Insects have only 6 legs. Insects have either 0, 2, or 4 wings. Insect wings attach at thorax.

Unit 2: Insect Anatomy   Page 11
I. Write About Wings
2-4, veins, wing cases, up and down
II. Mouth Match-Up
Fly mouth with soft food, ant mouth with plant leaves, mosquito mouth with blood, butterfly mouth with flower nectar
III. True or False
1. F,   2. T,   3. T,   4. F,   5. F,   6. F

Unit 3: Insect Life Cycles   Page 15
I. Life Cycle Line-Up
3, 4, 1, 2 incomplete; 4, 1, 3, 2 complete
II. Label the Caterpillar

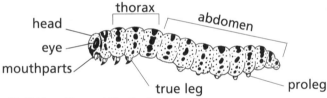

III. Write About Life Cycles
eggs, molt, metamorphosis, 4, larva, pupa, 3, nymphs, wings

Unit 4: Insect Survival   Page 19
I. Insect Survival Circle-It
1. b   2. d   3. d   4. c
II. Survival Tactic Match-Up
1. camouflage, 2. reproduction
3. body weapon, 4. escape
III. Survival Portrait
Answers will vary.

Unit 5: Water Insects   Page 23
I. True or False
1. T,   2. F,   3. F,   4. F,   5. T

II. Aquatic Adaptations
1. C   2. D   3. B   4. A

III. My Day Down Under
Answers will vary.

Unit 6: Spider Anatomy   Page 27
I. Spider Portrait

ocilli, eye, pedipalp, chelicerae, abdomen, cephalothorax

II. Spider Fact Circle-It
1. A 2. B 3. C 4. A
III. Insect and Spider Table

	Insects	Spiders
Number of legs	6	8
Number of body sections	3	2
Common number of eyes	2	8
Wings? (Yes or No)	Yes	No
Exoskeleton? (Yes or No)	Yes	Yes
Antennae? (Yes or No)	Yes	No
Molt to grow? (Yes or No)	Yes	Yes
Name of young when hatched	larva or nymph	spiderling
Arthropod? (Yes or No)	Yes	Yes

Unit 7: Spider Behavior   Page 31
I. Write About Silk
all, spinnerets, abdomen, egg, webs, dragline
II. True or False
1. T 2. F 3. F 4. T 5. F
III. Weave a Web

tangle web   orb web   sheet web

Further Resources:
Books: Age-appropriate field guides can be especially helpful to young naturalists. Two useful guides are *Children's Guide to Insects and Spiders* (Jinny Johnson, Simon & Schuster, 1996) and *National Audubon Society Pocket Guide: Insects and Spiders* (John Farrand, Jr., Knopf, 1995). Other invaluable books include *The Insect Book* (Connie Zakowski, Rainbow Books, 1997), *Kids & Science: Insects* (Ellen Doris, Grolier Educational, 1996), *Insects and Spiders: Reader's Digest Pathfinders* (Matthew Robertson, Reader's Digest, 2000), and the series *Insects Under the Microscope* (Tamara Green, Grolier Educational, 2000).

Internet Research: Several education programs, including the University of Arizona's Center for InsectScience and Colorado State University's Entomology Department, maintain Web pages. These sites often include photos, diagrams, and other visual aids. Links to on-line encyclopedias, databases, ongoing studies, and local entomology clubs may be helpful to teachers and students alike.